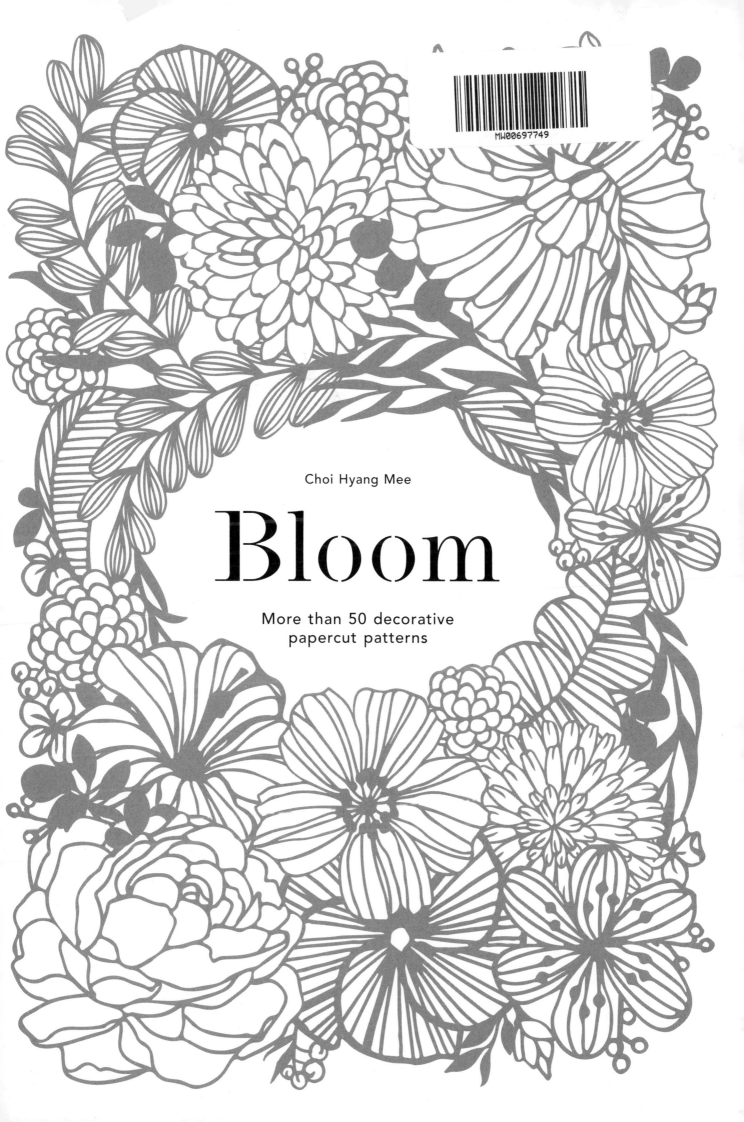

Choi Hyang Mee

Bloom

More than 50 decorative
papercut patterns

LAURENCE KING

Published in 2018
by Laurence King Publishing Ltd
361–373 City Road
London EC1V 1LR
United Kingdom
Tel: +44 20 7841 6900
Fax: +44 20 7841 6910
E-mail: enquiries@laurenceking.com
www.laurenceking.com

A catalogue record for this book is available
from the British Library

ISBN: 978-1-78627-167-9

Printed in China

A Note from the Author

Make a flower bloom from paper!

Are you worried that you might not be able to do it very well? Just follow the lines and cut – and it's done! It's so easy, you can do it whenever you feel like clearing your head or while listening to your favourite music. Or even while talking on the phone to a friend about a tiring day.

You may be wondering, "What if I overcut? What if I cross the lines?" No worries. It's okay. Really! It's okay. *Bloom* is full of flowers, grasses and leaves. Your cutting mistakes may create a better flower in the end. If the tip of a leaf gets cut by accident, it will still be a leaf.

Still discouraged? Not sure if you can complete the book? Remember, you don't have to do every design. If you make just one flower bloom, that's a complete work in itself.

What's most important is that you forget your worries and concentrate on cutting. Don't feel stressed out. Enjoy your experience with *Bloom*, and create your own masterpiece.

Shall we get started?

Choi Hyang Mee

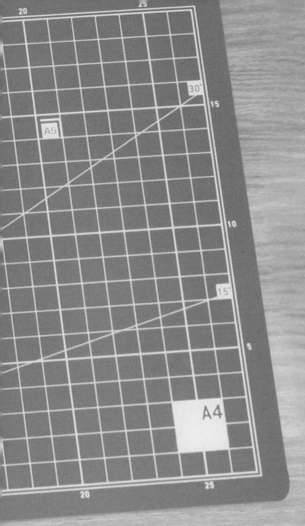

What You Will Need

Cutting Board/Mat
As the designs in this book have many fine details, the use of a rubber or plastic cutting board/mat is highly recommended. A soft mat is preferable to a hard one. Don't try to use a thick magazine or newspaper in place of a mat.

Art/Craft Knife
A knife (usually called an art or craft knife), available in art stores, is one of the best tools for papercutting, as you can cut with a similar sensation to drawing with a pen. There are many different types of knife, from the most basic pen-style ones, to ones with an awl-like tip, but any craft knife that feels comfortable in your hand will be fine.

Cutting Knife
While using a craft knife is recommended for papercut art, a cutting knife can sometimes come in handy as well. If you prefer using a cutting knife to a craft knife, it is recommended that you use a 30 degree blade. This is sharper than other general blades, and it will make it easier for you to identify and follow the lines of the pattern.

Scissors
While not essential, a pair of scissors is useful for trimming paper before working on the details of a pattern, or for cleaning up curved edges. A regular pair of paper scissors will do, or for more accurate cutting, use a pair of patchwork scissors, available from craft or haberdashery stores.

Masking Tape
It is easy to tear complicated sections of a pattern. They can get caught between the cutting board and your desk, or even in your hands. Prevent this from happening by placing masking tape on a section of the design before cutting. The adhesive on masking tape is not very strong so you can easily remove it after cutting.

Step-by-step Papercutting

1. Choose a design you like, cut along the cutting line to remove the page from the book, and place the pattern on a cutting mat.

2. Using your scissors, trim the paper around your chosen design. Make sure not to get too close to the edges of the pattern.

3. Using a knife, cut out the inner details of the pattern. Work on the smaller areas first, and then move on to the larger ones.

4. When you have cut out all the inner details, cut around the outline of the pattern. Move the knife as if you were "drawing" the outline.

5. Lifting out the finished piece may cause a tear. To prevent this, make cuts in four directions as shown. Cut from the widest points of the piece out to each edge of the paper, dividing the sheet into quarters.

6. Gently pull away each of the four quarters, while holding the design in place with your knife.

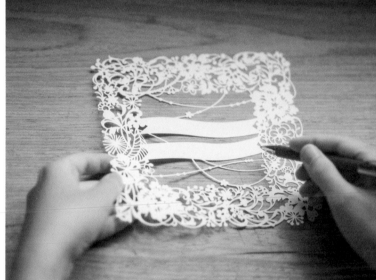

Please note:

The designs are printed on the reverse of the sheets, so you will need to flip the pattern after cutting to finish your papercut. For completed designs, see page 121 onwards.

Cutting line

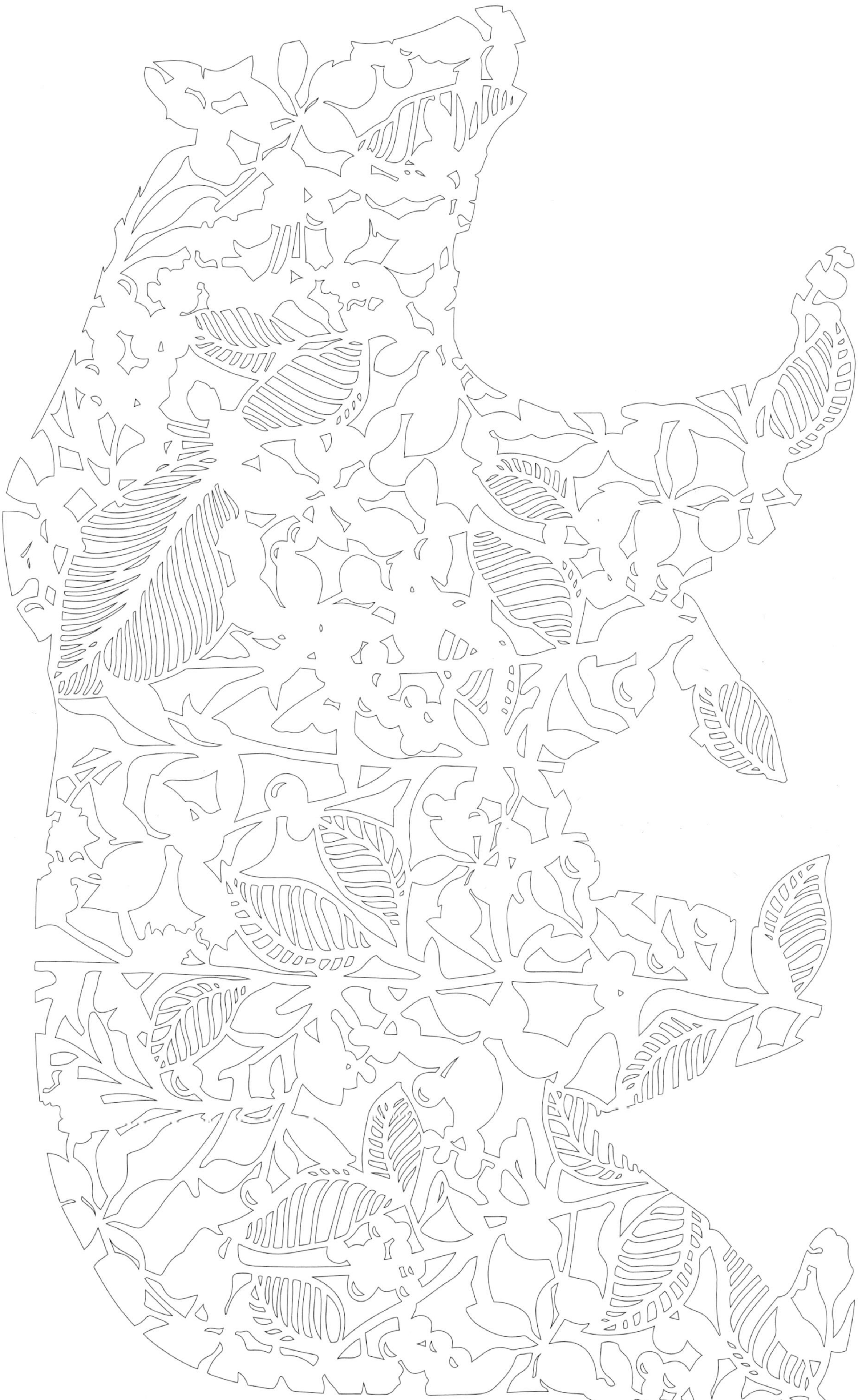

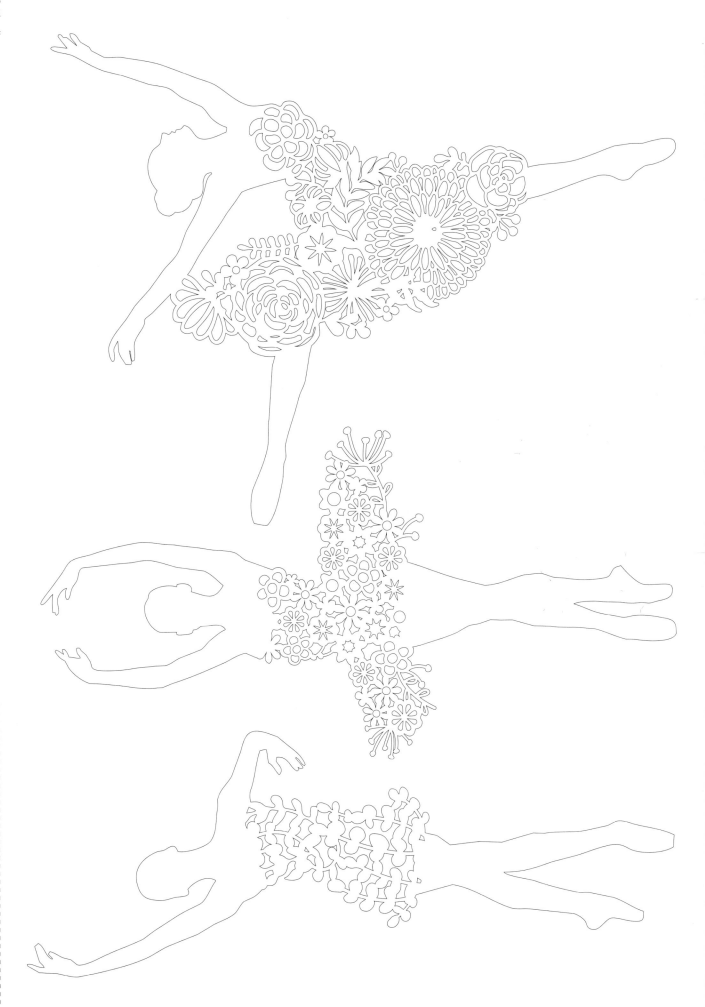

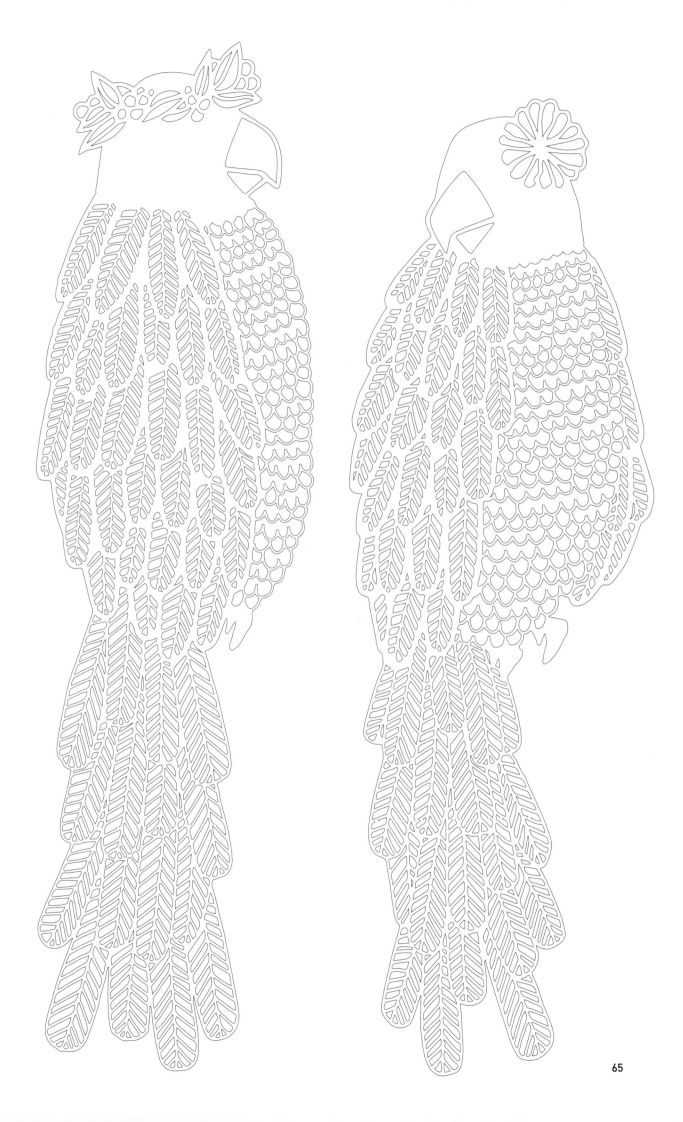

77

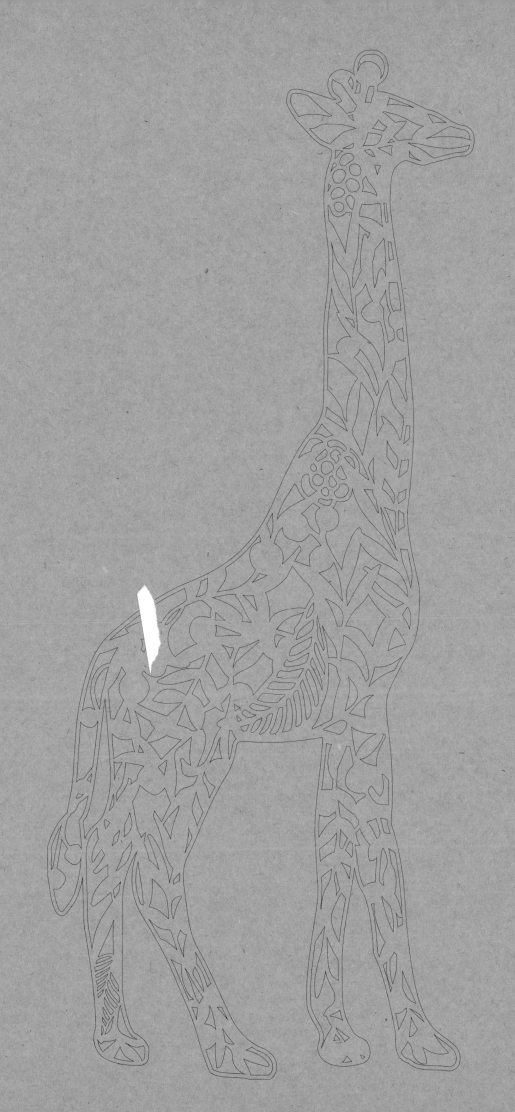

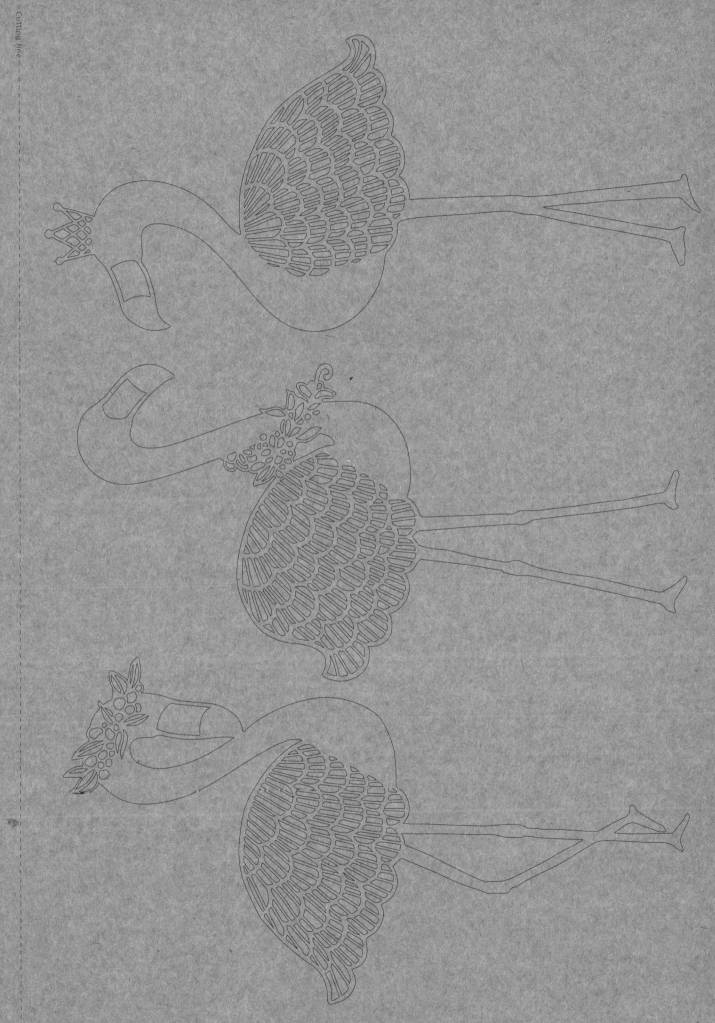

117

Final Pieces

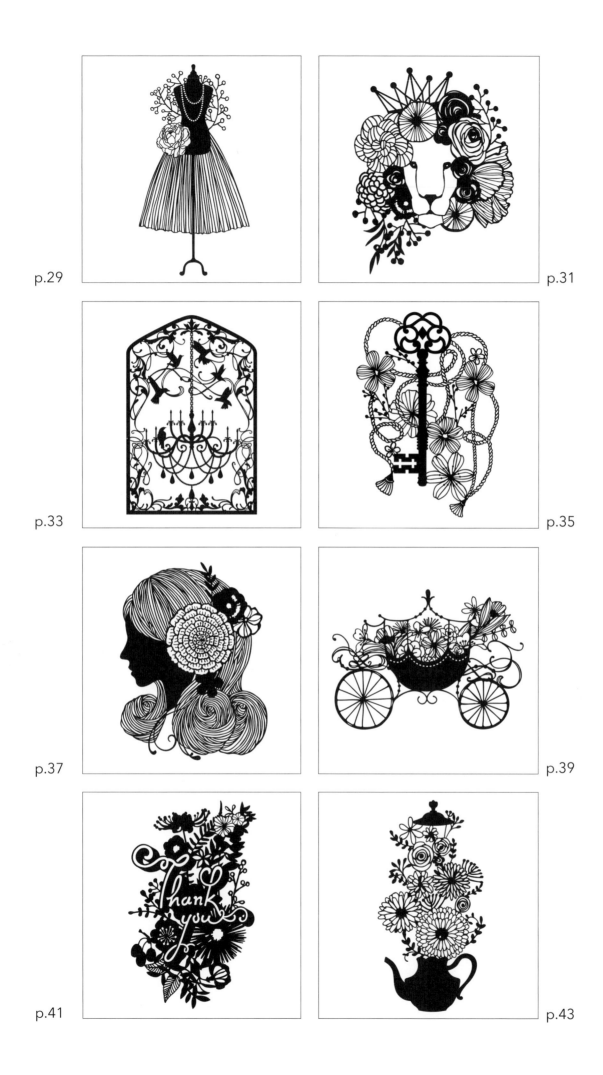

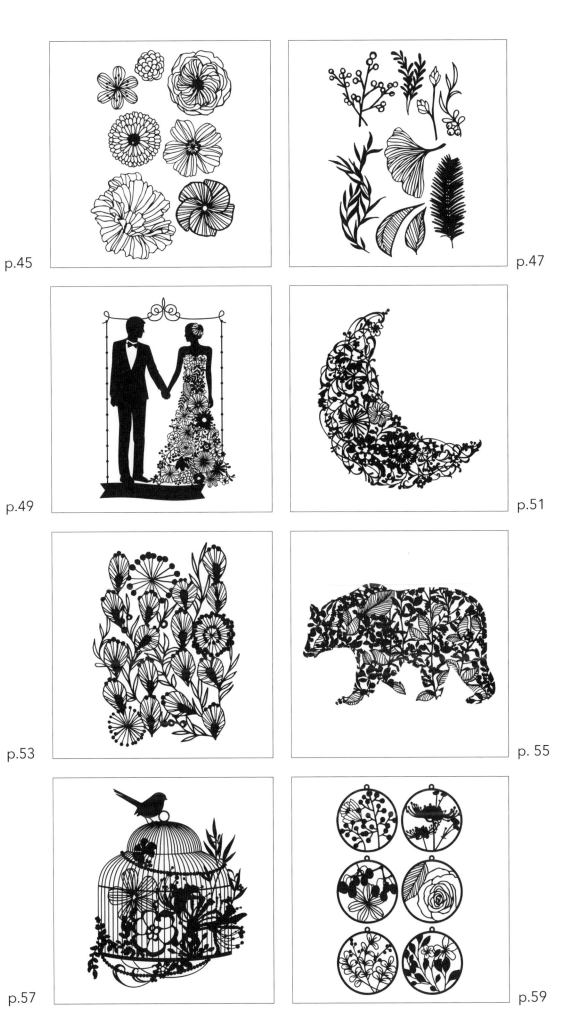

p.45

p.47

p.49

p.51

p.53

p. 55

p.57

p.59

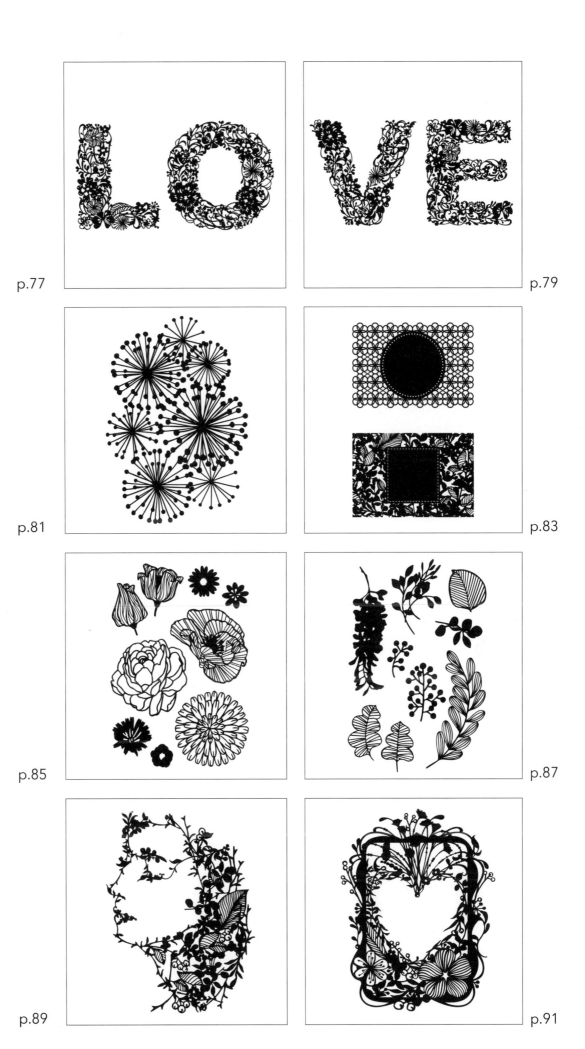

p.77

p.79

p.81

p.83

p.85

p.87

p.89

p.91

p.93

p.95

p.97

p.99

p.101

p.103

p.105

p.107

p.109

p.111

p.113

p.115

p.117

p.119

About the Author

Choi Hyang Mee has worked as a papercut artist since graduating from college, where she majored in industrial art. She loves to fill her everyday life with romance, and hopes that her papercut creations will bring happiness to many people.

Since 2015, Choi has published three papercut art books in Korea, starting with *Bloom*, then followed by *Bloom 2* and *Bloom 3*. In 2017, *Bloom* was published in Japan.

Before publishing her books, she collaborated with LG Household & Healthcare on package design for its premium skincare brand Sooryehan. Her works have also been featured by various media networks in Korea, including top magazines *Singles Wedding* and *Maison*, as well as in the 2015 New Year campaign for SBS, one of Korea's leading TV networks, and the online commercial for the 2015 Hyundai Card Fashion Week.

See more of Choi Hyang Mee's work on Instagram @nangmaner.